An Advent Study for Adults

Where Heaven Touches Earth

W0007056

Rob Weber

ABINGDON PRESS / Nashville

WHERE HEAVEN TOUCHES EARTH
AN ADVENT STUDY FOR ADULTS

Copyright © 2005 by Abingdon Press

All rights reserved.
No part of this work may be reproduced or transmitted in any form or by any means, electronic or mechanical, including photocopying and recording, or by any information storage or retrieval system, except as may be expressly permitted by the 1976 Copyright Act or in writing from the publisher. Requests for permission should be addressed in writing to Abingdon Press, P.O. Box 801, 201 Eighth Avenue South, Nashville, TN 37202-0801 or permissions@abingdonpress.com.

This book is printed on acid-free paper.

Library of Congress Cataloging-in-Publication Data

Weber, Rob, 1960–
  Where heaven touches earth : an Advent study for adults / [Rob Weber].
    p. cm.
  ISBN 0-687-74190-4 (alk. paper)
  1. Advent—Study and teaching. 2. Bible. N.T. Luke II—Criticism, interpretation, etc. I. Title.

  BV40.W36 2005
  263'.912'0715--dc22

                                                                2005016433

All scripture quotations unless otherwise noted are taken from the *New Revised Standard Version of the Bible,* copyright © 1989, by the Division of Christian Education of the National Council of the Churches of Christ in the United States of America. Used by permission. All rights reserved.

Scripture quotations marked (NIV) are taken from the HOLY BIBLE, NEW INTERNATIONAL VERSION®. NIV®. Copyright © 1973, 1978, 1984 by International Bible Society. Used by permission of Zondervan Publishing House. All rights reserved.

05 06 07 08 09 10 11 12 13 14—10 9 8 7 6 5 4 3 2 1

MANUFACTURED IN THE UNITED STATES OF AMERICA

To the congregation of
Grace Community United Methodist Church,
Shreveport, Louisiana,
to the children and youth in whom,
through eyes of active anticipation,
I see the amazing and unlimited work of God in the world,
to the entire congregation who inspires me,
prays for me, and understands my calling to teach and write,
sharing our ministry with the larger church,
to the staff who know what it means to do miracles
with loaves and fish,
and to those brothers and sisters who are still on their way . . .
the front porch light is on,
and the room is ready

Contents

Introduction

Michelangelo's Sistine Chapel painting "The Creation of Adam" has been reproduced all over the world. It appears in many forms in churches, living rooms, and restaurants. "The Creation of Adam" is a powerful and popular picture because it focuses on a dimension of reality that, as Christians, gives us our hope. It is a picture of the act of creation—of heaven touching earth. The beautiful event we celebrate at Christmas is another example of God's taking initiative and reaching out so that heaven would again touch the earth—the divine intersecting the daily. This picture of a touch from beyond has the power to shape the way we experience life in all our fears and joys.

For some reason, people have always looked to the sky as the place from which God would come to touch the world. The sky is so expansive and mysterious . . . and, even with airplanes, space shuttles, and space probes, still so beyond our reach. It is not in the farthest reaches of the cosmos, however, that we find the activity of God. It is in the activities that take place all around us that we are able to see most powerfully the continued touch of God on the world—if we have the eyes for it.

Our culture has made the Advent season a time of *physical* preparation for the celebration of Christmas that ends the day after Christmas. The decorations come down quickly so that we can move on to the next thing. But Advent is so much more than a time for lists, gifts, decorations, and Christmas cards. It is a season of rich, rhythmic preparation for our experience of the touch of God in the world today.

This is the beginning of the season of Advent. It is a time to celebrate the anticipation of the coming of God. Throughout this study, we will be looking at the ways in which we can become more aware of and more involved in where heaven touches earth around us, in us, and through us.

As a guiding image for our Advent journey this year, we will look in depth at one brief passage of Scripture found in Luke's Gospel. It is a small section of the Christmas story that opens up for us some important points of consideration and contemplation as we once again make this month-long journey to Bethlehem.

"Keeping Watch"

And there were shepherds living out in the fields nearby,
keeping watch *over their flocks at night. An angel of the
Lord appeared to them, and the glory of the Lord shone
around them, and they were terrified.*
—Luke 2:8-9 NIV, emphasis added

Compare the way our current culture celebrates this season to the way in which the church calls us to celebrate this season. On one side we are called to celebrate the season of Christmas, which, according to cultural tradition, starts the day after Labor Day. The beginning of this season is marked by several events. All of the gift items go on sale. All of the decorations go up in the malls and other public places. The background music in the stores changes from standard-issue elevator music to "It's the Most Wonderful Time of the Year." When this season begins, something deep happens within us—something almost as powerful as the dog's response when the behavioral scientist Pavlov rang his dinner bell. We hear that Christmas music and we find ourselves beginning to be drawn toward an inevitable buying splurge. The culture creates a season of preparation, but it is preparation for something very different from real Advent preparation. It is preparation to buy, to decorate, and to give. Cultural preparations for Christmas are not inherently bad, but let's not get confused and think that this is what Scripture is calling us to do.

The season we celebrate before Christmas in the church is not

11

called the Christmas season. It is called Advent. Advent is a time of preparation. It is the four weeks before Christmas Day. (It is a time when we prepare our hearts, our minds, our spirits, and all of our selves for the birth of Christ into the world.)

In one way, Advent preparation is kind of a strange thing to think about. For what are we preparing? Jesus has already been born, right? We know this from the Scriptures. The Scriptures tell us that he was born, died, and rose again. So, for what are we preparing? For what are we waiting? Is it the same dynamic as a birthday party—like a party for Jesus at which we get the presents? For what are we preparing at Advent? Jesus is here already.

Perhaps it will make more sense if we look at it this way: Even though Christ has come, and even though we understand that there is a God and that God is present, do you ever feel alone? Do you ever feel as if the prayers you are crying out are not being answered in the way that you would like them to be answered? Do you ever feel that you have questions that remain unanswered, so you sit and ask again and again, and all you get is silence? If so, you are not alone; I sometimes feel that way too. (The season of Advent is a shared experience that helps us see *the reality of living in a time in which Christ has come, but in which he is not yet fully revealed in our lives, in our minds, in our hearts, and in our world*) Advent teaches us the discipline and blessing of waiting on God. It teaches us active patience. The word *Advent* actually comes from the Latin *adventus,* which means "coming toward." Of course, we could look at Advent as our coming toward Christmas, but really, what we celebrate is God's coming toward us in the appearance of the Christ. This is a time to reflect on God's initiative of reaching out to the world—an initiative that is still underway. Advent is about learning to wait on the God who is constantly reaching out to us. As we begin our journey into this season, let's pay a visit to some shepherds who were living out in the fields near Bethlehem more than two thousand years ago.

Keeping Watch

What did the Scripture say the shepherds were doing? It said they were living in the fields, keeping watch over their flocks by night. They had to keep watch in this way because there were no electric fences to keep the jackals away from the sheep, and I'm fairly sure that sheep insurance wasn't available. If a wolf or some other predator killed their sheep, the shepherds were just out of luck—so they had to watch. If they lost those sheep (which provided wool, meat, and other important things that were needed and used), then they lost their very livelihood. The shepherds' lives and their families' lives would be gone. So they were out there in the fields at night, watching in order to protect the things that kept them alive.

One common image of the shepherds in Luke 2 is a picture of them on a hill with a big full moon, stars in the sky, with a light illuminating the field and their surroundings. But they didn't have halogen lights on their four wheelers. They didn't have big streetlights. They didn't have floodlights to keep the coyotes away. And at times they didn't even have the moonlight to rely on. It was dark for those shepherds. So how did they keep watch? They *listened.*

It wouldn't have gone well for those shepherds if they all had decided to hang out in the fields with their digital music players, passing the time listening to music. Why? Because if they had done that, then when the coyotes came and ate the sheep, the shepherds wouldn't have heard what they were "watching" for! They would have missed it. They could have had their eyes wide open but missed it. Why? Something would have obscured their ability to keep watch with their ears. By filling themselves with noise and information, they might have missed what they were placed in the field to do.

I don't know about you, but I feel as though I do that often. I wake up, turn on the TV, the radio, the CD player, or the computer, and as the morning goes on, my ears are filled with whatever happens to be on. Music, phones, people, and all kinds of things are going all day long, and it's constant, constant, constant—until I get home at night. Then at home, I'm talking, telling stories, checking in with family, doing homework, preparing dinner, making plans for the next day, listening to the news and other nighttime TV shows before getting into bed. If I am not careful and intentional about it, the only time I get silence is when I go to sleep. Do you ever feel like that?

Let me ask you this. If it had been possible for those shepherds to become distracted from their task, to become unaware of the dangers that were threatening their sheep—if it were possible for distraction or inattention to obscure their silence, causing them to miss what they were waiting for, is it possible that the same thing can happen to us? (The main question for us is, how can we wait effectively and hear the renewed coming of God today if we don't allow ourselves to be silent?)

In college I used to hitchhike to a monastery. I liked to stay with the monks every once in a while. These were Trappist monks. They wore black and white robes. They baked bread. They gardened. They raised bonsai trees. They did very normal things, but there was a noticeable difference: They did all of these things in silence. They would not speak except in confession, during a time of teaching, or in an emergency. Most of the time, everything they did throughout the day was done in silence.

This type of silence is a very different experience from what I am used to. When I went to the monastery usually I was so stirred up on the inside, my brain was so filled with information and sound, that it took about three days for my inner being to become still enough to let go and abide in God's presence. Silence, for me, took getting away. At first making the adjustment to silence was difficult, but then it became something I craved. I would spend my entire day in silence with the monks, my silence broken only as we worshiped five times a day. I loved to enter the arched, cathedral-like chapel, which was illuminated only by a couple of candles, to sing psalms responsively. The only sounds I had heard all day had been either the sounds of nature or the sounds of the psalms echoing from the voices of monks who had stopped and stilled their souls long enough to listen. For me, the monastery became a place where heaven touched earth.

Of course, not all of us can just pick up and go off to a monastery for silence and reflection. We have responsibilities at work, at home, at church, and at school. (But the possibility of seeking silence and an opportunity to listen is available for each of us. It is a choice. I invite you during this season of preparation, this season of Advent, to see if you can set aside some time away from distraction, away from noise, away from craziness, just to be still. Perhaps you could simply light a candle at home, get quiet, and sit in silence, listening for God.

Actively Anticipating

Imagine that as those shepherds were keeping watch in the fields, sometimes the full moon would be out, and stars would flood the sky.

14

Sometimes, however, clouds obscured the light. Sometimes the shepherds could see more clearly, and sometimes they would have to make an extra effort to focus so they could see or hear if their sheep were starting to wander off, or if some coyotes or other dangers were approaching. The shepherds had to keep a direct watch, a careful watch, an intentional watch, over those sheep.

We do some intentional watching too. We intentionally watch TV, setting the digital recorder or the VCR to record our favorite shows. We intentionally watch our young children at the swimming pool to keep them from harm. We watch the stock market. We watch for that special piece of mail. We watch for new business opportunities. Watching is active anticipation, and the way we watch shapes the intensity and reality of what we perceive.

The shepherds were intentionally watching for the negative things that might endanger the sheep. Sometimes we take this same approach when we look at life. Take, for example, the way we sometimes approach relationships. Maybe you have been burned before in a relationship, so that you carry with you a negative outlook. Then the opportunity for a new relationship presents itself, and this could be a great person, but you've got this negative focus, and you think to yourself, *I know this is too good to be true. I know this person is going to do something to mess it up, so I'm going to watch carefully. I'm not going to get too close or too involved. I won't be too quick to place my heart in this person's hand, even though things seem great now. I'm not going to do that, because I know that something bad is bound to happen.* And so you watch, and then when the slightest thing happens (and it's going to happen, because everybody is imperfect), you see it magnified all out of proportion. If you are watching for it and it comes, it might have been just some tiny little breach. But because you waited and actively anticipated, it appeared huge, and it colored the entire relationship. The closer we watch, the more prepared we are, the greater the experience when what we are expecting arrives.

In Advent, the same principle is at work. Advent is about actively anticipating the touch of God in the world. I once saw a little sign that read, "The universe is filled with miracles and surprises simply waiting for our wits to become sharp enough to notice them." Elizabeth Barrett Browning wrote, ("Earth's crammed with heaven, / And every common bush afire with God; / And only he who sees

15

takes off his shoes; / The rest sit round it and pluck blackberries") (*Aurora Leigh,* Book vii).

Not long ago it was reported that there would be a meteor shower visible in our part of the country at three a.m. My family and I set the alarm clock and arranged lawn chairs out in the yard. When the clock awakened us, my wife, my son, and I stumbled out of bed, made some hot chocolate, wrapped up in blankets, and went outside to look at the sky. We sat in silence watching the night sky. Then, it happened—like distant skyrockets, meteorites skipped across the earth's atmosphere. Sharing in that moment of preparation, silence, anticipation, and experience of a celestial phenomenon made us aware of the depth and the grandeur of the universe, and it brought us closer together. The way in which we prepared to watch affected who we are as individuals and as a family.

The truth is that the presence of God is all around us. Christ is already present, yet not fully revealed. God's touch is happening now. Becoming aware and watching for the presence and the touch is what Advent is about. Advent is a time for actively watching for the touch of God in your life.

Developing "Advent Eyes"

People marveled when professional cyclist Lance Armstrong broke a long-standing record by winning the Tour de France for a sixth con-secutive time. When interviewed about his incredible feat and how he was able to accomplish the task, which had included a particu-larly challenging trek through mountainous regions, Armstrong replied that he had trained for the race by riding in the Rockies. If you can climb the Rockies, you can climb anything, he said. His prowess on race day had come from his preparation. He had needed to develop not only stamina, focus, and balance, but also superior muscles for climbing hills.

Likewise, as we prepare in this season of the year for the coming of Christ, we choose to listen and to actively anticipate his coming; and by so doing, we develop eyes that are able to see. We develop "Advent eyes."

A couple of years ago, as we were preparing for Advent at Grace Community United Methodist Church in Northwest Louisiana, we wanted to help the children of the church develop eyes that watched for the presence of God around them. We gathered a group of second- through fifth-graders and formed what we called the "Children's Worship Team." The object was to help these children begin to look at the world actively, watching for the presence of God, and ask them to consider, as they watched, how they might share what they saw with others. On one occasion, members of our children's worship team went out to be "God reporters." They were given little disposable cameras and a list of questions asking, "Where do you see God loving, God's people serving, God's people giving, God's Creation, and beauty in creation?" During the next week, the children went out taking pictures with eyes that were actively looking for God. As they looked, they began to see the answers to their questions because they were actively anticipating. They were developing "Advent eyes," eyes that anticipate the coming of God. They were looking for where God is already active in the world.

On another occasion, the children painted pictures of how they might describe God's interaction with humanity. One child painted a picture of the Holy One juggling the universe. Maybe it's God, maybe it's Jesus (because there are holes in the feet), or maybe it is both. Out of the mind of a fifth-grader came an image of the juggling Creator Redeemer. That is a beautiful and complex image of who God is, who the Divine One is, and how the divine touches our lives—the juggling Creator Redeemer, seen in the heart and mind of a child. Active anticipation leads to the development of Advent eyes.

As we prepared for Communion during the Advent season, the children gathered in the church kitchen and made bread. They mixed flour, milk, and other ingredients in the food processor and made a huge ball of dough. They put it on the counter with flour spread all over the place. They made a mess, but it was a holy mess. The children kneaded the dough. (We added yeast, but the bread became unleavened because they pounded on it so hard that the yeast died, or at least gave up. The bread turned out somewhat tough, but *they*, the children, had made it.)

Afterwards, still covered with flour, as the bread baked and the wonderful smells filled the kitchen, we sat down to remember the stories of bread that showed God's provision and connected the Christ child with the Jesus of the communion table. We talked about the Israelites in Egypt who cried out to God because they were enslaved, and how God sent Moses to them. We remembered the evening when the angel of death moved throughout Egypt but "passed over" the Israelite households that were marked with the sign of the Lord, allowing for the freedom of the Israelite people—the Passover. When it came time for the Israelites to leave Egypt, Moses said, "It's time to go! We've got to get out of here, now!" They didn't even have time to put yeast in the bread before they left, so it was unleavened.) We talked about the Hebrew people wandering in the desert, without any food or a snack truck following them around. There wasn't much to eat in the desert, but God provided bread—manna from heaven. We talked about Jesus gathering with the disciples around a table and their celebration of that same Passover with unleavened bread. Jesus took that moment and incorporated all of history and their entire story and told his followers that the story is no longer just about the past, but "This is my body, broken for you, and my blood which is poured out for you. Every time you eat this bread and drink this cup, remember me."

After the stories, we went into the worship area and practiced serving communion. We practiced breaking the bread, holding it, looking into people's eyes, and saying, "This is the body of Christ, given for you." We held the cup and said, "This is the blood of Christ, shed for you." These are our children, and now their eyes have been changed. They probably never will be able to see a piece of bread in the same way. They never will be able to go into a church and experience a service in the same way. Now, they see with Advent eyes. My hope is that this season, all of us will see with Advent eyes as well—actively listening and watching.

He is come, and yet he is not fully arrived. We wait on God with Advent eyes. As we actively anticipate God's touch, we become witnesses to the constant reality of the divine initiative—God coming toward us. As we wait, as we watch, we will see that this is a place and a time where heaven touches earth.

Questions for Reflection and Discussion

1. How is your preparation for Christmas shaped by our culture? How is it shaped by Scripture and by your faith?
2. What do you think is meant by "active patience"? Explain the term in your own words.

3. The author describes days that are filled with constant activity and a barrage of information, days in which he experiences silence only when he goes to sleep. How does your experience compare to this description of life?
4. What does it mean that Christ has come, yet is not fully revealed in our lives, our minds, our hearts, and the world?
5. Light a candle and spend five minutes in pure silence, listening for God. What do you hear?

Prayer

Help me, God, to stop. Help me be still in your presence. The tasks on my lists can wait. The only waiting that really matters right now is my waiting on you. Still my mind; quiet my soul. Touch my eyes so that I may see you as you continue to come into the world today.

Focus for the Week

This week, focus on Advent as the discipline of keeping watch for the coming of the Christ who is here, but is not yet fully revealed.

"*Peace*"

*"Glory to God in the highest heaven,
and on earth **peace** among those whom he favors!"*
—Luke 2:14, emphasis added

Advent is a time when we prepare for the coming of the Prince of Peace. We are preparing, yet we know the truth is that he has already come. Jesus has arrived. Jesus came more than two thousand years ago, he arrived in Bethlehem, and we still celebrate this occasion. It is nice to know that God sent the Messiah, the Prince of Peace, to be with us. And it shows, too, doesn't it? The Messiah, the Prince of Peace, has ushered in a whole new time of peace. There is peace in the world. There is peace in all of our relationships. There is peace in all of our homes. There is peace all over the place. Isn't that nice? It is something to celebrate—

Wait a minute. There is not peace. There is not peace all over the world. There is not peace in all of our homes. There is not even peace in all of our hearts. So did the Prince of Peace not bring what was expected?

Maybe we must look more closely at the message proclaimed by the angels. "Glory to God in the highest heaven, / and on earth peace among those whom he favors." This seems a little confusing as well. Are the angels saying that it is those who have God's favor who get the peace? In other words, if you don't have peace, then that must mean you don't have God's favor. Can that be right? I have

21

known a lot of people who are very close to God who have not known peace; so is that what the message in Luke 2:14 means—if you don't have peace, you don't have God's favor? I don't think so.

Jesus said, in John 14:27, ("Peace I leave with you; my peace I give to you. I do not give to you as the world gives. Do not let your hearts be troubled, and do not let them be afraid." Jesus talked about a different kind of peace. He also talked about God's peace that passes all understanding. So, what is that peace?

The peace of Christ takes on different forms. It comes in forms that are evident if we open our eyes and see a type of peace that is beyond normal human understanding. It is a peace that is available to each one of us, a peace that can sustain us, and a peace that can move through us. (God gives us the gift of peace, and we respond by both accepting the gift and emulating the giver in sharing and spreading that peace to others.)

Peace with God

You probably are familiar with the story of Creation, from the book of Genesis. God made the world. God made people. People lived in the garden. They could do anything they wanted, except for that one thing God told them not to do. And what did the people do? They did that one thing. Then they tried to make excuses, but that didn't work. Out the door they went.

Ever since then, they have been having a problem—*we* have been having a problem—called sinfulness, self-centeredness, non–God-centeredness, doing our own thing instead of God's thing. Even though we try—*OK, God, I'm going to be better, I'm going to do better, I'm going to follow you*—still we mess up. We have this broken relationship with the Creator. The Scriptures tell us that God has tried time and time again to bring us back—first, through laws. God basically said, "I'm going to give you ten. Stick with these ten, and you'll be OK."

"OK, Lord," we said, "we're going to stick with these ten, and—oops! Sorry!"

"OK, maybe I need to get a little more specific. Let me give you all this stuff in Leviticus. I'll be more specific as to how you are to behave."

That didn't work either. We kept falling, we kept failing, and we still fail today.

There is a breach between the One who is "God in the highest heaven" and those of us who dwell on earth. The question is, how is that breach to be healed? How is peace to be restored? It won't happen by our trying to "get back to God." Our efforts are not sufficient to cross this breach. Healing happens as God comes to us in the form of Jesus Christ, the child who entered into the world, born here so that God's grace and love could cover us, make us new, and restore our hearts to peaceful relationship with the Creator. Peace with God. That's the first part of the peace brought by the Prince of Peace. That is the central message of the gospel.

Maybe you have heard that message but haven't experienced its reality in your own life. Perhaps you are struggling with something you have done, or with something you haven't done, or with something you keep doing, or whatever it might be, and you wonder, *How can I come to God? How can I be at home with God when I'm dragging all of this brokenness around?* Hear this: The message of the gospel is that God knows your life, and God loves you tremendously. That is why God sent Jesus to bring you peace. It's there for you. What is required is simply opening your heart to receive that gift of grace and the peace that it brings, to allow Christ to come in, to cleanse you, to give you a new beginning. That is the first kind of peace that the Prince of Peace brings. It is a peace that is beyond our understanding. It is a peace that is not like what the world gives. It is the peace that can come only through Christ. This is an ongoing process. We receive the grace that has come, but it is not yet fully revealed in and through our lives. Advent is about preparing for and receiving a deepening experience of this revelation of grace.

Peace from Knowing We Are Not Alone

There is another kind of peace as well. Even when we have been restored, even when we have been forgiven, even when we have accepted Christ and received a newness of life and a new beginning, we don't always experience peace.

Have you ever felt that you are getting closer to God, but then you fall down just as hard as, if not harder than, before? Have you ever felt as though things are falling apart all around you? Have you ever come to your senses and asked, *God, how did I create this mess,* and you don't know what to do? There is no peace when you are in that kind of mess. That's a feeling of *peacelessness.*

Consider another person who was a child of God, chosen by God, blessed by God, who found himself in a very difficult situation. His name was Jacob. Jacob had a twin brother named Esau. Of the two brothers, Esau was the more rugged. Esau was the hunter, the outdoorsman. As the firstborn son, Esau was due to receive his "birthright" or inheritance, and his father's blessing. Esau was supposed to be the one who would lead the family upon his father's death.

Jacob, however, had a different plan in mind: Jacob was going steal his brother's birthright. He was going to claim for himself the blessing that was due to Esau.

You might deduce that Jacob wasn't a very nice guy. He took advantage of the fact that his father was very old and was blind. Jacob put on goatskins so that his smooth neck and hands would feel hairy like the neck and hands of his brother, and he went in to see his father. "Give me the blessing, quick, before you die," Jacob basically said. And just like that, Jacob has stolen Esau's birthright, he steals Esau's blessing, and then he leaves town in a hurry. Why? Because Esau is a big, hairy guy, even without the goat skins, and he's coming after Jacob.

So Jacob hits the road, running across the desert through the emptiness. While he is running, he is exposed and isolated. There's not a comfortable rest area with clean restrooms. There is no express hotel. He's just out there in the desert. Jacob couldn't carry camping gear with him; he had to leave too quickly to gather supplies. He is being pursued by his brother, who looks like a professional wrestler. Jacob is out in the middle of the wilderness surrounded by jackals, snakes, scorpions, and wolves, and he has no place to sleep.

Jacob is heading toward a place called Paddan-aram, in hopes of staying with his uncle, Laban. He has broken ties with everything he has ever known. I imagine Jacob remembering the places where he grew up, remembering being close to his family, being cared for by his mother and father. He has left all of that behind, and now out in the middle of nowhere, without even a sleeping bag, he rests his head upon a rock and realizes how broken and alone he is.

For Jacob, there is no peace. There in the desert, alone, underneath the stars, with his head upon a rock, pursued by a troubled past and running into an unknown future, Jacob falls asleep. While he is asleep, God, that same One who much later would pierce the night sky to tell the shepherds of the coming of Christ, pierces the darkness in Jacob's mind, evoking the image of a stairway where heaven touches earth, where angels are ascending and descending, and the Lord comes and stands beside Jacob and says to him, "Know that I am with you and will keep you wherever you go. . . . I will not leave you" (Genesis 28:15). When Jacob wakes up, he thinks, *Even with all of this in my past, even in the face of an unknown future, even with this brokenness right here and right now, with my head upon a rock, I am in the very presence of God, and I didn't even know it!* (See Genesis 25:19-34; 27; 28:1-22.)

That knowledge didn't change Jacob's situation. It didn't stop Esau from pursuing him. It didn't make the rock soft against his head. It didn't get Jacob a free ride to a certain place of blessing. *But it did give Jacob the knowledge that he was not alone, and that he was dwelling in the very presence of God, even in the midst of his struggles.* And that is peace. Not peace like the world gives, but peace like God gives.

I remember back in the third year of starting our church, we were trying to construct a church building, but rain delays were causing big problems, the necessary funds were not coming in as needed, and I discovered that some people I thought were friends were trying to undermine our efforts. During this time, my wife's mother fell and broke her leg, so my wife and our three-year-old son went to Memphis to take care of her for several weeks. In addition to that, I received a call from family members in Atlanta informing me that my mother's lung was bleeding, and that she might have cancer.

That was a lonely time. I found myself wondering what I was doing in this situation, and wondering where God was. I prayed for strength and I looked for answers, but none came. Finally, when I felt there was nothing else I could do, I reached out to God and said, "Hold me." And God did. Jacob said, "Surely God is in this place, and I didn't even realize it." *God's peace comes to us to let us know that even in seemingly peaceless times, we are not alone.*

Peace God Brings Through You

Peace-bringing does not stop with peace being brought to us. The same God who wanted to restore the breach between heaven and earth, who sent a child to be with us, to give us grace and bring us back into relationship, that same One who pierces our darkness and says, "Even though you are struggling, I am with you," wants to say "Peace" to *all* who sit in darkness.

Do you know how God plans to do that? I'll let you in on a little secret: That's what *you* are for. Feel your hands holding this book. Those are the hands that the Creator of the universe wants to use to bring hope and healing to people. Feel that beating of the heart in your own breast. Yours is the heart that God wants to use to stir, to quicken, to bring light to those who dwell in darkness in your very town or community. God is still in the peace-bringing business. The announcement now comes to those who have been redeemed. And you know what? That announcement is for you.

(One of the most powerful experiences of heaven touching earth is found when God enables you to be a peace-bringer) Ask the children in the church who were given the opportunity to bring shoeboxes filled with gifts for people they didn't even know. On a rainy, muddy, cold day, they traveled to a little community not far from the church. This is a community where the poverty stands in stark contrast to the surrounding neighborhood. Church members spent the day cleaning the park, repairing homes, and helping in whatever ways they could. At the end of the day, in an old house that had been donated to be a community center, the children brought out the shoeboxes filled with gifts and distributed them to other children who perhaps otherwise would have received nothing for Christmas. I watched the eyes of the children as the gifts were shared. Those opening the gifts received them with excitement and joy, but perhaps even more joyful were the children who brought the gifts. In that act of peace-bringing, peace came to everyone there, and as we shared in that experience, heaven touched earth—and continues to do so.

The story of the Scriptures is a story that begins in Genesis with the gift of a peaceful world. The unfortunate turn of events very early on in the story is the loss of peace through human sin. Sometimes the headlines show us a world that reflects too clearly that loss of peace, and yet we must always remember that God's constant activity throughout the Bible, as well as through the lives of the faithful, is to seek to restore that peace. Sometimes we get so caught up in the fear and anger surrounding the tensions of our world that we become vengeful and ready to respond to hate with hate. The God who pursues us—the same Prince of Peace—reminds us of our calling as Christians: "Blessed are the peacemakers" (Matthew 5:9). Peace among people in the world isn't just something to hope for, pray for, and work for because it makes us more secure and protects our way of life. It is something to hope for, pray for, work for, and commit ourselves to because it is God's will for us.

I received an e-mail not long ago that had an attachment. I downloaded the file and found that it contained pictures of a wheelchair ramp. Why? There was a woman in the church whose mother couldn't access her house because she had fallen and hurt herself. So church members went over there and built a ramp. They didn't build a ramp just for her to get *into* her house, they built a ramp so she could get into her house *and* so she could access the backyard, which is where she loves to spend her time. Now what was that all about? That's about God taking people here and now and reaching divine hands into our bodies and using us like gloves to touch earth and bring peace. Peace . . . not like the world knows; peace that can come only through Christ.

That is what God wants to do through us. The Prince of Peace has come to provide a restoration of that breach between heaven and earth, reminding us that even in difficulty we are not alone, and calling us to be more than we ever could be on our own, to be ones through whom God's hands touch, ones through whom heaven touches earth.

Questions for Reflection and Discussion

1. How have you experienced God's peace in your life?
2. Have you ever experienced peacelessness? Reflect on and describe this experience.
3. Can you think of a time when you shared Jacob's perspective that "Surely God is in this place, and I didn't even realize it"? Reflect on and describe that experience.
4. What particular peaceless situations in the world today cry out for a touch from God?
5. Light a candle and spend five minutes in silence, listening for God. What do you hear?

Prayer

God, make me attentive to the reality of your peace. Let me experience it in my soul and in my life. Help me be a conduit for your peace, allow heaven to touch earth through me today. Amen.

Focus for the Week

This week, reflect on and pray about God's peace in and through our lives.

"For All the People"

*In that region there were shepherds living in the fields, keeping watch over their flock by night. Then an angel of the Lord stood before them, and the glory of the Lord shone around them, and they were terrified. But the angel said to them, "Do not be afraid; for see—I am bringing you good news of great joy for **all the people.**"*
—Luke 2:8-10, emphasis added

In the first week of Advent, we examined the story of the shepherds keeping watch. In the second week, we studied the way in which the message of peace proclaimed to the shepherds is still a message of peace for us today—peace with God, peace in God, and the peace God brings through us. This week, we will look at the message the angels brought and explore what it shows about the direction and availability of the grace of God.

My "Us and Them" Tendency

Not long ago, I was coming home from an out-of-town trip. It was a time of heightened security. As I walked through the airport, terrorism news alerts were playing on the TV monitors. People were anxious. Soldiers with automatic rifles were posted in key spots. As

I approached the security clearance area, I had to stand in a long line, take my laptop computer out of its case, and practically undress. Then I had to run my belongings through the X-ray machine before walking through the metal detector. I thought, *I can handle this heightened security because I want to be safe.*

After clearing security, I found out that my flight was delayed. Then the next flight was delayed, and also the next. Finally, they called for boarding. I got in line, waiting to get on the airplane. By now, I was on the second leg of the flight. I had already been on one airplane and had shown my identification. I had my boarding pass and my frequent-flyer card; everything was ready. I approached the gate agent and handed her my boarding pass. Just then a large, uniformed security agent came over to me and said, "Sir, we're going to have to take you over to the searching area." I began to grumble internally.

At the search area, I had to empty everything out again. Security staff went through everything with rubber gloves. They dug through everything I had. I even had to take my belt off to ensure that it did not conceal a knife. I walked out of there thinking, *I thought it was just suspicious, weird-looking people they stopped and searched.* But security is for everybody (including the suspicious, weird-looking people like me!).

That was a strange situation. I wouldn't have thought for one moment that I would have been picked out, taken out, or isolated. I was looking for the people "you've got to look out for." You know— *them,* not *me.* We have a tendency to think of ourselves—whoever we might be or from wherever we may come—as "the ones"; that is, "chosen," "special," or "set apart." But the Scripture in Luke 2:8-10 has something to say about this particular tendency.

A Message for All People

"Choose your audience" proclaims a commercial currently running on cable TV, encouraging people to consider cable as a medium for their advertising message. The proposed benefit is the ability to spend advertising dollars more effectively by targeting the appropriate market segment. For example, you can choose to tailor your message directly to fifty-year-old bald guys who watch golf and who are interested in weight-loss products, the stock market, and hair-loss prevention. In sharp contrast in Luke 2:8-10, though, God's message was targeted to the shepherds that evening, but it wasn't for them alone.

God's message that came through the angels to the shepherds said, "Don't be afraid. We've got a message, but don't think it's only for you. We're not singling you out; it's for everybody." God let the shepherds know that the message was for all people. And although this message was first delivered more than two thousand years ago, this is still true of God's message today. It is a message that reaches different people—people who are young, people who are old, people who look different from one another, and people who have grown up in different backgrounds. God's message is for everyone.

There is a lot of separation between people, depending in part on their place of origin and culture. God has created us in tremendous diversity. We are very different from one another, but we are all creatures of God's hand. God's message isn't only for me, for "my" people; it is for the entire diverse family. Sometimes, sadly, and perhaps too frequently, we forget this.

In one church I served, I wanted to do a mailing to the community to invite those who were not part of the church to participate in our Vacation Bible School. My plan was to mail the invitation to every person within our ZIP code. When I brought the plan up for approval (it required funding that was not in the current budget), many in the meeting were excited about the possibilities for outreach. Some were slightly hesitant because of the uncertainty of planning and hosting an indeterminate number of new people. But one man was concerned for a different reason. "Preacher," he said to me, "if you mail this invitation out to the whole ZIP code, you are opening up a big can of worms." What I believe he meant was that "those people—the ones on the other side of the tracks—live in this ZIP code as well."

Now, to me, having been given the task of becoming a fisher of people, I think "opening up a big can of worms" might have been just what we needed. According to my reading of the Scripture, heaven doesn't touch earth selectively—it touches it all over. Jesus himself related to all people. Jesus, the Word made flesh, lived out the inclusive direction proclaimed by the angels on that dark night. No one was too far gone for him. Jesus spent time with people at the Temple, with prostitutes on the street, and with a woman who touched him because she had been suffering and bleeding for so long. Jesus went to the man who was blind and touched his eyes. He had lunch with the tax collector who abused his power and made money through exploiting the people. Jesus traveled with those who used to spend every day fishing. It didn't matter who they were or from where they came; through Jesus, the love of God reached out to *all* of them—to all people.

A Community for All People

As we prepare our hearts during this Advent season for the coming of Christ, it is important to ask, "What does it mean for that message to come through us to all people, now? What does that mean for me? What does that mean for my church community?" The direction of that message still has to do with how we prepare to receive as well as how we prepare to reach out. I'll sum it up in one word: *hospitality*.

The Hebrew people in the Scriptures were reminded to be ones who welcomed and ones who participated in hospitality because they heard over and over, "Remember that once you were strangers and aliens and foreigners. Remember what that was like? So welcome the stranger, the alien, and the foreigner."

Sione is one of the pastors on staff at the church I serve. He is a good friend and a deeply spiritual man. He is originally from Tonga, a country of islands near Fiji, very close to the International Date Line. Sione shared with me a story that has shaped his expression of hospitality and welcome. After moving to the United States, and shortly after the birth of his son, he and his wife went looking for an apartment in a community to which they were moving. They found an apartment that was convenient for work and school and they inquired about renting it. The owner of the apartment, seeing that Sione and his family were non-white, constructed some reason why they could not rent the apartment. Sione was angry over this discrimination, but more than that, he felt hurt as he held his child and imagined what his son might encounter growing up because of the color of his skin. This kind of experience can make for bitterness, or it can inspire the development of a deep attitude of hospitality and acceptance of people from different backgrounds or cultures. I am so thankful that the Christ in Sione has enabled the second response.

The feeling of wondering whether you will be accepted, welcomed, judged, rejected, or ridiculed lives strongly in so many people beyond the walls of the church. They may not even be from another country or cultural background; diversity in background, perspective, and experience comes in all forms. Many churches have considered how to be more hospitable as congregations with "Open hearts, open doors, open minds." We have ways to welcome visitors and ways to register their attendance. We have put the coffee on and spruced up the foyer. We may even have made the worship-service bulletin easier to read, or the location of the nursery easier to find. Creating a church, however, where heaven touches earth in the model of Christ, also means *making room for those who are not like "us."* What about the person whose skin is a different color from yours? What about the single parent, the unwed mother, the recently incarcerated, the addict, the AIDS patient, or the AIDS widow or widower? What about the person with multiple body piercings or the person who has no clean clothes? The question for us this Advent is, *How are we preparing our hearts and our churches to provide a welcome for all people? How are we becoming a community through which heaven touches earth more fully?*

Reaching Out to Christ

When I went to serve my first church, I met a man who was very ill. He was in the process of dying in his home. I visited with him frequently. Sometimes his wife would visit with us, and sometimes I would sit with him as she left the house for a while to run some errands. I loved being with this man and listening to his stories. Toward the end of his life, he gave me a little book of Tolstoy's writings that had meant a great deal to him across the years. He pointed out one particular story and said, "Read this one, 'Where Love Is, God Is.' This is the story that taught me how to love."

The story was about Martin the cobbler. Martin is an old man who has become isolated and embittered, even angry with God, because of the death of his wife and their last remaining child. Since the time of their deaths, Martin has ceased to interact with the people of the town or to share in their celebrations, and instead he throws himself completely, day and night, into his work repairing shoes.

One day Martin hears a voice speaking to him as if in a dream, and informing him that the Christ will be coming to visit him that very day. Martin doesn't completely believe what he has heard, but nonetheless, he begins to watch and work in a different way. As he watches for the coming of the Christ, he begins to notice people's struggles outside his shop window. He notices Stepánitch, a poor old man, freezing outside while trying to shovel snow. Martin brings him in from the cold, offers him hot tea, and treats him with kindness.

Later in the day, Martin notices outside a frail woman with a baby, and both are wearing only summer clothes. Martin brings them in from the cold, gives them something warm to eat and drink, and offers the woman his coat to keep her warm.

Finally, Martin overhears a disturbance outside between a young boy and an old woman selling apples. The boy had stolen an apple from the woman because he had no money and was hungry. Martin breaks up the disturbance and becomes the peacemaker between the two.

Later, as the sun begins to set and the cobbler prepares to stop work for the evening, he again starts to despair. *I thought the Christ was coming to visit me!* he thinks to himself. Just then a voice comes to him, and says, "I did come to visit you, Martin. I was the man whom you brought in from the cold and gave something warm to drink. I was the woman whom you fed and to whom you gave your coat. I was the hungry child to whom you gave nourishment. And I was the old woman and the young boy who were fighting in the street, and to whom you brought peace. Whatsoever you have done unto the least of these, my brothers and sisters, you have done unto me." (This story was written in 1885. This English translation from Leo Tolstoy, *Walk in the Light and Twenty-three Tales* [Farmington, Penn.: Plough, 1999], pp. 143-53.)

If we watch for people as we would watch for Christ and realize that in welcoming others we are welcoming Christ, we will be well on our way to living out the love that is *for all people*. This is really what Advent is about—not presents and decorations, not even manger scenes, candles, and wreaths, but learning to make room in our hearts, minds, lives, and churches to wait and watch, with active anticipation, for the coming of the Christ who was, who is, and who is yet to come.

Questions for Reflection and Discussion

1. If someone who is seeking, hurting, hoping, and wondering if they will be received and welcomed came to your church or to your home, what would they discover? Explain your answer as fully as possible.
2. In what ways, and to what degree, are you open to diversity?
3. If you were in the author's position, how do you think you would respond to the comment, "Preacher, if you mail that invitation out to the whole ZIP code, you are opening a big can of worms"?
4. How does heaven touch earth, through us, for all people?
5. Light a candle and spend five minutes listening for God. What do you hear?

Prayer

O God, teach me to love others as you have loved me. Give me a hospitable heart, and help me be open to learning from those who are not like me. I long for a life filled with your compassion. Amen.

Focus for the Week

Advent calls us to develop a spirituality of hospitality. This week, reread Luke 2:8-10 and reflect on how God's message is for all people. Ask God to open your eyes and your heart to new ways of being a welcoming servant to others.

"For You . . . This Day . . . a Savior"

In that region there were shepherds living in the fields, keeping watch over their flock by night. Then an angel of the Lord stood before them, and the glory of the Lord shone around them, and they were terrified. But the angel said to them, "Do not be afraid; for see—I am bringing you good news of great joy for all the people: **to you** *is born* **this day** *in the city of David* **a Savior,** *who is the Messiah, the Lord. This will be a sign for you: you will find a child wrapped in bands of cloth and lying in a manger." And suddenly there was with the angel a multitude of the heavenly host, praising God and saying,*
"Glory to God in the highest heaven,
and on earth peace among those whom he favors!"
—Luke 2:8-14, emphasis added

For the past three weeks we have been looking at this Scripture and asking, *What does it mean today, and how can we prepare for God's entry into and through our lives?* During the first week of Advent we examined keeping watch, being attentive to what God might do, to what God is doing now, here, and to the way in which God keeps being born anew all around us. In week two, we studied about a message of peace in a time of very little peace. There is peace with God, peace in God even in difficult situations, and the peace that God brings through us, as we become agents of God's reconciliation and peace. Last week we explored how the gospel—the good news of Jesus Christ—is not isolated just to people who look like we do or who think as we do or who live in a certain time or place, but is instead a gospel made available to all people. This week we will focus on the announcement of Jesus' birth. The message that came to the shepherds that evening was beautifully simple: *to you, this day, a Savior.*

Let's explore the three sections of this message.

For You . . .

Sometimes it seems that we understand the story of Christ's coming into the world. We know the drill. We can sing the hymns. We can even get that certain feeling as all the people in the church light candles one after another and "Silent Night" is sung unaccompanied. We know the words, the familiar rituals, the smells, the meals, and the music, but sometimes the reality of the coming of Christ seems like something very distant, something almost unreal—something to remember, something from another time that happened to other people—and we wonder, *What does that have to do with me . . . really?*

There are two words spoken to the shepherds that night that have something important to say in answer to that question. The message was, and still is, targeted: *For you . . .*

As a child, I remember looking under the Christmas tree during the days before Christmas, watching as different gifts were added from different family members and friends from around the country. It was exciting to see those colorful packages being added one by one to the shining spectacle of the Christmas tree, and it was even more exciting to see that some of those gifts had my name on them. These days, I still enjoy watching the nest of colorful boxes fill the corner by the fireplace, under the tree, but now I get more excited about sneaking in surprise gifts and watching the others' faces as the surprises are opened. On Christmas morning, it is our son's job to read each tag and deliver the gift to the recipient. "Here's one for

Grandpa from us!" "Here's one for you, Dad. It's from the dog!" The gifts are sorted, distributed, and opened. It matters whose name is on the little tag, doesn't it? In Luke 2:8-14, the words "to you is born" tell us the name on the tag of the gift God has given to the world.

Their personal encounter with the angels as well as the personalized message the angels brought probably had a powerful effect on the shepherds' lives, don't you think?

I had an angel experience once. A local church held a live Christmas exhibit each year as part of their celebration of Advent and Christmas. The setting was elaborate, consisting of a living Nativity scene with full-scale buildings, costumed actors, dramatic lighting, and live animals. The setting had been developed with the purpose of transporting people back into the time of Jesus. I walked through the scene, intrigued by the tax collectors, the priests and teachers at the Temple, the beggars, the children in their homes doing chores, and various other vignettes of ancient Bethlehem.

As I rounded one corner near the end of the exhibit, I found myself looking at the Nativity scene. It was beautiful. Framed by a rustic stable, there stood the Holy Family. Joseph stood beside Mary (the girl playing the part was all of about thirteen years old), who was sitting on a little stool beside the manger, with a little baby Jesus in her lap. This was a real baby, too. He was fussing a bit, which added to the reality of the situation.

Also part of the same scene, but cast in a different kind of light, were the angels. One young angel was in the stable with the family, looking on adoringly as the mother held the child. Another angel stood just outside the stable, almost as if on guard against anyone who would try to come in and harm the baby Jesus. One angel, by some elaborate means, was hovering above the stable, with huge, lifelike wings.

I stood transfixed. I had imagined the picture before. I had looked at hundreds of little manger scenes made of porcelain, glass, or olive wood, but seeing it live and in person—up close—gave me a completely different perspective. I stood there in somewhat stunned silence, probably with my mouth slightly agape and with moistened eyes.

After a while, I realized that I needed to move on so the people behind me could continue through the exhibit. As I turned to go, something a little strange happened. All of the actors remained in character except for one of the angels. The one standing at the manger, looking adoringly at the baby Jesus, nodded at me. It felt strange, but what was I to do? I nodded back. I continued to move on, and the angel followed. He came to the edge of the scene and stopped me, saying, "Wait, Rob—I never got a chance to thank you for being in the room when my mother died."

The angel knew my name. I was reminded of the way in which God touched the earth so long ago. I was reminded, through the way the angel spoke to me, of the way in which God still touches us and touches through us. It was a two-way street. God was present in the angel's speaking to me, and I had been present in this angel's life, allowing me to be a hand of comfort and a touch of presence in a very difficult time.

Because God has come, there was, and there is, a place where heaven meets earth for me and for you. Heaven touches earth; it touches you, it touches me, and it continues to touch through us. Those two simple words spoken to the shepherds are still being spoken, for the message is *for you.*

Today . . .

Do you ever find yourself living somewhere other than in the present? Maybe you live in the Land of Unreleased Regrets. Perhaps you live in the Archives of Past Wrongs and Problems. Maybe you live in the misty plains of If Only. Or could it be that your time is spent just over the horizon of Someday? Is that just a part of getting older?

Seeing children so excited about preparing for Christmas is very different from the harried looks I see on the faces of so many adults this time of year. Maybe it's that way with *you* this season. Are you concerned about the gifts that are yet to be purchased? Are you anxious about cards, letters, or other communications you have yet to send? Are you nervous about money or what's in the news or the gatherings that you have or haven't been invited to? Do you find yourself thinking about this season being over so that you can get on with life? That's the difference between making Christmas to-do lists and developing Advent eyes. Those lists involve things that will be done at some other time. The sensitivity of Advent eyes is directed to the next word those angels delivered: *today.*

When my son Jonathan was just six months old, I moved my family to a new city to start a church. Because there was no congrega-

40

tion, there was also no parsonage. We found a little 1,200–square-foot house to buy, and we moved in. It was a little bit of a fixer-upper, with turquoise appliances, brown and turquoise paisley wallpaper, and turquoise "sparkle" counters, which sported knife marks, coffee stains, and cigarette burns displaying years of age. The most important room for us, however, was the nursery. We wanted to have the nursery "fixed right" for our new little gift from God. In our previous parsonage, we had very carefully prepared one of the bedrooms as a nursery, in anticipation of the birth (not knowing, of course, that we were about to be moved to start a new church). We wanted the nursery in this new house to be ready for our new boy as well. We painted the room, set up the furniture, hung the pictures, and put up the shelves for books, toys, and stuffed animals. There was a large, wide, floor-length window on the front wall of his room. This window looked out onto a front yard shaded by huge branches of two sprawling live oak trees. It was a peaceful place and a good room.

As the days and weeks went by, Jonathan grew, my work got busier, and I began to focus my energy, efforts, and attention on what was to come with the new church we were trying to start. I had to work toward those distant horizons of what could be and try to convince as many people as possible to come with me. Things got hectic. I became consumed in the frantic activity of ministry and especially with the extra energy, creativity, and endless contacts involved in starting a new church from scratch. As time went on, even though my body lived in the present and I slept at my house, my mind was somewhere else. I was living in the future, focused as well as possible on seeing a dream and a calling become reality.

After a while, our little one began to speak words. His sounds of playing or crying that drew us down the hall each morning took on new dimensions. It became almost a ritual each morning for several months. The silver shafts of the rising sun peering over the horizon would find their way through the clusters of oak leaves and slip lightly through the blinds on the window, splashing the wooden floor with silver and pink. As Jonathan's eyes responded to the luminous intrusion, his mind would rouse from sleep and move into consciousness. His eyes would open and see the miracle of the new day that was happening. Motivated by the powerful and beautiful events transpiring all around him, he would pull himself up in the crib, survey the situation, and as if he were calling the new day into existence, announce, "I wake up! It's the day!" Sleepy parents, called into being by his proclamation of the existence of a new day, would appear like magic to greet him. As I greeted him, standing in his bed with his long, blond curls still dancing the dance of bed hair, I saw the wonder and immediacy of his being completely in the moment. "It's the day," I would say back to him. He reached out his arms for me to lift him from the confines of his crib and as I held him, my angel reminded me of the importance of *today*.

Our lives run at full speed so much of the time, we find ourselves living somewhere other than in the moment God has given us. Sometimes, as were those shepherds, we are blessed by being divinely interrupted and we are reminded of the preciousness and the fleetingness of *today*.

I read of a man who experienced one such moment while watching TV. He heard on a television newscast that it had been ten years since the *Challenger* spacecraft disaster. It was nothing more than a casual comment, but the fact struck him like lightning. This man said that in an instant, it became painfully clear to him that those ten years had gone by in a flash. He wondered how many more ten-year stretches he had left in his lifetime. Yet in those years since the disaster, he had constantly mortgaged his happiness to the future in favor of "I'll sit back and enjoy life when . . ." *When?* When the next business deal comes through? When this or that legal mess gets cleared up? When finances are more secure? *When;* always *when*. But in that moment of clarity, my friend was graced with wisdom: He had no guarantee of the next ten *days*—let alone ten years. "It's as if the moment was written in blood," he said, "'If you are ever going to get around to [living fully] you'd best get at it" (Earnest Larsen, *Overcoming Depressive Living Syndrome* [Liguori, Mo.: Triumph, 1996], p. 12).

There is something about the word *today* that speaks to us. The word today reminds us that God isn't some old story. God isn't merely memory, or a human construction. God enters into life in someone's *today*. Heaven touches earth in the here and now.

A Savior . . .

Think for a moment about the shepherds on the evening of the delivery of the angels' message. They didn't get what they were expecting, either experientially or conceptually.

The delivery of this message was the best thing that could ever have happened to them. The Creator God parts the curtains of space and time and enters into their moment of reality to tell them, "To you this day is born a Savior." That's good news! And how do they respond? They are terrified! And the angels knew it, too. The first thing they said was, "Don't be afraid." Right! Imagine what it was like being those shepherds, minding the sheep in the quiet countryside, in the cool of the evening, when suddenly, there are glowing, hovering beings coming at you out of the sky! I can imagine the shepherds' hair standing on end, their staffs dropping, and the sheep running and scattering. "<u>Don't be afraid</u>"—<u>right</u>! Angels showing up like that in the middle of the night was *not* what they were expecting; neither was the message they received.

These shepherds surely knew the story of the Creator God. They knew they were part of the people of God. They also knew that they were without much power, smelly, and marginalized. These shepherds and others, who had for so long been awaiting a savior, were waiting for someone who would free them and their society from the domination of the Romans. They were looking for some tax relief and religious freedom. They were living in a time of a widening gap between the haves and the have-nots. The haves controlled the political process and the power. The have-nots were being taken advantage of and were losing what little they had. Quality education was available only to the wealthy or the well connected. The shepherds on the edge of town would have embodied the situations and the wishes of many throughout the Israelite society. They wanted a savior to ride in on a white horse, someone who would lead a revolution to overthrow the oppressors and bring back dignity and order to a society that was humbled and broken. However, they didn't get what they expected. They wanted to be saved from oppressive social conditions by the establishment of a new earthly kingdom. But the salvation announced by the angels was different. The shepherds expected a warrior. Instead, they got a baby.

Even though the announcement the shepherds received was not what they expected experientially or conceptually, something happened that evening that really changed their perspective. They became aware of the story in a different way. The story became real to them, and it changed their lives. It was a message of the Savior bringing transformation of life and direction, not only to them, but

43

also to the entire world. God had pursued them and had spoken to them about the One foretold by another angel: "She will bear a son, and you are to name him Jesus, for he will save his people from their sins" (Matthew 1:21). This is not simply a message of individualistic salvation and personal holiness. It is so much more. Through Jesus, we are saved:

- From trusting in the powers of this world rather than in the power of God
- From the tendency to focus on self will rather than on the will of God
- From brokenness and disobedience
- To live in newness of life here and in the life to come

God entered into this time, space, and flesh for a reason. God came to give us not only a way out of this life, but also a way into it—fully. This was not what they expected.

Now, if this really is more than simply a story on a page, then the implications of this message should have a profound effect on all of us. *"Born to you."* The words spoken to the shepherds two thousand years ago were not for them alone. They echo forth across the ages and leap again from the printed page to the heart, and they reach out to you as you hold the pages of this book. You. Yes, *you*. This is no old story that is relived once a year in dusty memory, in colorful preparation, or in the fragrance of evergreen and cinnamon. It is a living story calling you to enter into it again and to receive the gift, tagged with your name. *Today*—this moment—all we have. *The Savior*. We are gifted by God with grace, new beginnings, and a promise of eternal hope, and we are called to live fully and abundantly in this moment—this ongoing gift of life. For you . . . today . . . a Savior.

And you . . . seated on the hillside of your life . . . waiting, preparing, and watching with Advent eyes . . . do you hear the hovering of the angels' wings? Listen closely, for the One who was, who is, and who is to come, even now, is coming toward you.

Questions for Reflection and Discussion

1. What would change in your life if angels appeared to you today and reminded you of the birth of the Savior?

2. What is meant by the statement, "God came to give us not only a way out of this life, but also a way into it—fully"?
3. In what ways do you "mortgage your life to the future"?
4. Is there something that is keeping you from hearing and responding to God's calling for you today? What are you waiting for?
5. Light a candle and spend five minutes in silence, listening for God. What do you hear?

Prayer

God, I wait for you with an open heart. Remind me of your love for me. Surprise me today with your grace and give me eyes to see you. Save me from my busyness, and set me free to live this gift of life fully—for you. Amen.

Focus for the Week

This week, reflect on and pray about how the coming of the Savior is a personal and present reality, and how truly receiving the Savior has dramatic consequences in our lives.

AUTHOR ROB WEBER says that Michelangelo's Sistine Chapel painting "The Creation of Adam" "is a powerful and popular picture because it focuses on a dimension of reality that, as Christians, gives us our hope. It is a picture of the act of creation—of heaven touching earth." The author says that the beautiful event we prepare for during Advent and celebrate at Christmas—the birth of the Christ Child—"is another example of God's taking initiative and reaching out so that heaven would again touch the earth: the divine intersecting the daily. . . . Throughout this study, we will be looking at the ways in which we can become more aware of and more involved in where heaven touches earth around us, in us, and through us."

This four-week study, appropriate for both group and individual use, provides one lesson for each week of Advent. Each lesson focuses on a portion of the Christmas story scripture from Luke 2:8-14 and includes questions for reflection or discussion, a brief prayer, and a focus for the coming week.

ROB WEBER is the senior pastor and founder of Grace Community United Methodist Church in Shreveport, Louisiana. Grace Community is a teaching church, with creative multigenerational ministries that serve over 1,200 in worship attendance each week. Rob Weber wrote and hosted the video segments in *Beginnings: An Introduction to the Christian Faith* (Abingdon Press). He also is the author of *Visual Leadership: The Church Leader as Imagesmith* and *Reconnecting: A Wesleyan Guide to Renewal for Our Congregation*, and is the coauthor of the *Communion* volume in the *Igniting Worship* series (all Abingdon Press).

 Abingdon Press

Cover design by Roy Wallace III
Cover art by Smithsonian American Art Museum,
Washington, DC / Art Resource, NY

GENERAL INTEREST / SEASONAL / ADVENT

0687741904 N ADVBK   1 @ 5.50
WHERE HEAVEN TO